# THE POWER THAT IS WITHIN

## Becoming the Woman God Designed You to Be

# THE POWER THAT IS WITHIN

## Becoming the Woman God Designed You to Be

By

Minister Moira Boakai

(Author of Diary of a Pastor's Wife)

Anointed Rose Press Publishing™

Anointed Rose Press Publishing™

---

# THE POWER THAT IS WITHIN©

- **Bec**oming the Woman God Designed You to Be –

Copyright©2026 by Moira Boakai

PHONE: 1(302)561-0963
EMAIL: moira.boakai@gmail.com

**The Power That Is Within / Moira Boakai**
*(trade paperback: alkaline paper)*

ISBN 13:979-8-9993069-6-8
LCCN: 2026904704

Motivation / Religion

---

Cover Designed by Moira Boakai
Publisher: Anointed Rose Press
Email: septembersummer09@gmail.com
**1(484)378-0939**

# Dedication

To every woman who has ever felt unseen, unheard, or unworthy — this book is for you.

May you rediscover your divine strength and rise boldly in the power God placed within you.

...Moira

# Table Of Contents


Copyright ------------------------------------------------------ iv

Dedication ------------------------------------------------------- v

Table of Content----------------------------------------------- vi

Foreword----------------------------------------------------------viii

Preface ----------------------------------------------------------- ix

Acknowledgment------------------------------------------------ xi

Introduction ---------------------------------------------------x1

Prologue ------------------------------------------------------x11


## CHAPTERS:


1.There's More Inside You Than You Realize --------------- 1

2. The Voice of Doubt vs. The Voice of God ---------------- 5

3.Breaking Free from Fear and Comparison------------------13

4.Activate Your Anointing------------------------------------18

5. From Brokenness to Boldness-------------------------------25

6. Faith Over Feelings, Walking in Truth, Not Emotion----32

7. Purpose Over Pain, Turning Your Wounds into
Wisdom -------------------------------------------------39

8. Becoming Her, The Woman God Designed You to Be--45

9. When the Fire Refines, Not Destroys ---------------------52

10. The Voice of Purpose, Hearing God's Direction for Your
Next Season -------------------------------------------59

11. Rise and Reign — Walking in Spiritual Authority and
Confidence -------------------------------------------------66

12. The Power of a Transformed Mind — Living Free from
Limiting Thoughts -------------------------------------73

13. When God Seems Silent — Trusting His Timing in the
Waiting------------------------------------------------------80

14. Peace Over Pressure — Finding Rest in a World That Never Stops ----------------------------------------------------------- 87

15. Walking in Wholeness — Healing Your Heart, Spirit, and Soul ----------------------------------------------------- 94

16. Reigniting Your Fire — Staying Spiritually Strong When You Feel Empty --------------------- 101

17. Carrying the Light — Becoming a Vessel of Hope and Influence --------------------------------- 108

18. Becoming Unstoppable — Walking Boldly in Destiny Without Fear--------------------------------- 115

About the Author ----------------------------------- 122

# Foreword

"The Power Within" by Minister Moira Boakai is much more than an inspirational book. It is a powerful tool which reaches to the common thread that we as women of all ages, nationalities, cultures, social or economic status, and spiritual status deal with in our very core – the frequently gut-wrenching internal questions of "Who am I?"; "What is my true purpose in life?" and "Does anyone truly see and understand the real me?

Yes, we live out and perform our multi-faceted roles and functions such as wife, mother, daughter, sister, girlfriend; and walk through our careers and professions with various levels of success or distress. Yet underneath it all, there are times and seasons that come into our lives when we struggle with fear, pain, anxiety, a sense of inferiority, comparing ourselves to others, brokenness, woundedness and much more.

Minister Moira shares wisdom and insight from a biblical perspective that every woman can relate to of how to "grow" through and not just "go" through these seasons, while becoming the awesome woman that God has designed each of us to be. We are each designed to be beautiful, powerful, fruitful and victorious. Get your copy and you will be blessed.

Pastor Vicki Warner
New Life Evangelistic Ministries
Pennsylvania

# Preface

Many people spend their lives searching for strength, direction, and purpose without realizing that the very power they are seeking already exists within them. "The Power That Is Within" is not just another inspirational book—it is a spiritual awakening.

This book was written for anyone who has ever felt overwhelmed by life, uncertain about their future, or discouraged by the challenges they face. It is for those who feel there must be something greater inside of them, yet they do not know how to access it.

Inside these pages, you will discover that God has already placed within you a divine strength, wisdom, and authority that can transform your life. Through biblical truth, personal insight, and spiritual encouragement, this book will help you:
• Recognize the power God has already placed inside of you
• Develop a deeper understanding of your spiritual identity
• Overcome fear, doubt, and limitations
• Walk confidently in your purpose and calling
• Strengthen your faith and relationship with God
• Discover the courage to rise above life's challenges

What makes this book unique is that it does not simply motivate you, it awakens you. It reminds you that the power you are searching for is not outside of you. Through Christ, that power already lives within you.

If you are ready to step into a new level of faith, confidence, and spiritual authority, then this book will help guide you on that journey.

My prayer is that as you read these pages, you will begin to see yourself differently. You will realize that you are stronger than you thought, more capable than you believed, and more powerful through God than you ever imagined.

The power is already there. Now it is time to discover it.
— **Minister Moira Boakai**

# Acknowledgments

To my children, you are my greatest blessings and inspirations.

To my readers — daughters of faith across the world — thank you for walking this journey of healing and empowerment with me.

*...Moira*

# Prologue

Deep within every woman lies a divine strength----a power placed there by God Himself. "The Power That is Within" is a heart-felt and faith-filled journey that invites women to re-discover who they are in Christ and to embrace the beautiful and purposeful life He has designed for them.

Through personal reflection, biblical truth and empowering insight, Minister Moira Boakai guides you to break free from fear, insecurity, and doubt. She reveals how to tap into your inner strength, renew your mind with God's Word, and walk boldly in your true identity as a woman of faith. So, whether you are navigating challenges, seeking spiritual growth, or longing to live with greater purpose, this book will awaken the strength that already resides in you -- the strength to overcome, to rise, and to shine for God's Glory. It's time to unlock, "The Power That is Within".                    ... Moira

# Chapter One

## *There's More Inside You Than You Realize*

There comes a time in every woman's life when she looks in the mirror and barely recognizes the person staring back. She has survived heartbreak, betrayal, disappointment, and seasons she once thought she'd never endure. She has carried others on her back while silently breaking inside. She has smiled through tears, prayed through pain, and showed up even when her strength was gone.

But the truth is you are not empty. You are not forgotten. You are not weak. You are powerful. Not because of who you are on your own, but because of Who lives inside of you. There's a power within you that hell cannot destroy and life cannot make silent. It's the power of the Holy Spirit, the strength of divine purpose, and the resilience of a woman who refuses to quit. This book was born out of my own battles, the moments when I questioned God, doubted my worth, and almost lost myself trying to please people who couldn't see my value. It was in those broken moments that God whispered, "Daughter, I placed power inside of you long before you were wounded. You just forgot it was there."

**"The Power That is Within"** is not just a motivational book, it's a spiritual awakening.

It's for the woman who's tired of being stuck, tired of feeling invisible, and ready to rise again. It's for the one who knows there's more to her story but doesn't know how to reach it.

Through faith, healing, and divine empowerment, you will learn to:

- See yourself the way God sees you.
- Rise above pain, fear, and insecurity.
- Reclaim your power and walk boldly in your purpose.
- Transform every trial into a testimony of victory.

God is about to awaken the power within you. Not the strength that comes from striving, but the supernatural strength that flows from surrender.

So, take a deep breath...wipe your tears, and get ready to rediscover the woman you were always meant to be...powerful, fearless, and full of divine fire.

**Welcome to your new beginning.**

# My Personal Notes

# Chapter Two

## *The Voice of Doubt*
## *vs.*
## *The Voice of God*

There's a war that happens inside every believer — not with swords or armies, but with words. It's the battle between the voice of doubt and the voice of God.

One tells you, "You're not ready."

The other says, "I've already equipped you

One whispers, "You'll fail again."

The other declares, "You can do all things through Christ who strengthens you."

This inner conflict determines not only how you see yourself but also whether you'll step into the destiny God has prepared for you.

❖ When Doubt Speaks Louder Than Truth

Doubt rarely shouts; it whispers. It disguises itself as logic, fear, and self-protection. It tells you to wait until you feel ready, until people approve, until life looks perfect.

But the truth is you'll never "feel" completely ready for what God has called you to do. Faith doesn't wait for perfect conditions; faith moves in obedience even when everything looks uncertain. When God called Moses, he doubted his voice.

When He called Gideon, he doubted his strength. When He called Esther, she doubted her timing.

Yet every one of them discovered this truth:

❖ **God doesn't call the qualified — He qualifies the called.**

So, if doubt is speaking, it's a sign that purpose is near. The enemy attacks what threatens his agenda. He knows that if you ever believe God's truth about yourself, you'll walk in unstoppable confidence.

❖ Recognizing God's Voice.

The voice of God doesn't condemn you; it convicts you with love. It doesn't remind you of who you were; it reminds you of who you're becoming. It doesn't make you anxious; it gives you peace even in uncertainty. Jesus said, "My sheep listen to my voice; I know them, they follow me."—John 10:27

That means you can learn to tune out the noise and hear the gentle whisper of the Spirit within you.

❖ How do you recognize His voice?

• Through His Word -- it never contradicts Scripture.

• Through His peace—even hard instructions come with calm assurance.

• Through His timing -- He confirms His will again and again in quiet ways.

When you spend time with God, you begin to know His tone and the warmth, the mercy, and the power. You'll start to recognize that still, small voice that says, "Daughter, you can."

## ❖ Silencing the Inner Critic

The loudest enemy we often face is our own self-talk—that every "what if." But you can't walk in divine power while agreeing with lies. Every time doubt speaks, respond with truth. When doubt says, "You're not enough," declare, "God's grace is sufficient for me." When fear says, "You'll fall again," remind yourself, "The Lord upholds me with His righteous right hand."

You don't fight doubt with emotion — you fight it with the Word. "Faith comes by hearing, and hearing by the Word of God." — Romans 10:17

The more you feed your faith, the quieter doubt becomes.

## ❖ A Shift in Identity

Every time you choose to believe God's voice over doubt, your identity strengthens. You begin to see yourself as chosen, not overlooked; powerful, not broken; and loved, not forgotten.

The same Spirit that hovered over chaos in Genesis now hovers over your life bringing order, healing, and new beginnings. When you say "yes" to God's truth, you silence every other voice that tries to hold you back.

❖ Prayer of Activation

Father, I thank You that Your voice still speaks to me today. Teach me to discern Your truth above every lie. Silence the noise of fear, insecurity, and doubt that tries to steal my confidence. Let Your Word anchor me when my emotions waver. I declare that I will no longer follow the voice of doubt; I will follow the voice of destiny. In Jesus' mighty name, Amen.

❖ Declaration of Power

- I recognize the voice of God in my life.
- I will not be led by fear, doubt, or insecurity.
- I am guided by the Spirit of truth, filled with divine wisdom, and grounded in peace.

- *God's Word defines me, strengthens me, and empowers me.*

❖ Closing Thought

The next time doubt tries to whisper, "You can't," remember — heaven has already said, "You will."

_______________________________________________

_______________________________________________

_______________________________________________

_______________________________________________

_______________________________________________

_______________________________________________

_______________________________________________

_______________________________________________

_______________________________________________

_______________________________________________

_______________________________________________

_______________________________________________

# Chapter Three

## *Breaking free from fear and comparison*

Fear And Comparison Are Silent Thieves.

They don't always come through the front door; sometimes, they slip quietly into your thoughts, making you question your worth, your timing, and even your calling.

Fear says, "What if I fail?" Comparison whispers, "She's doing it better than me." And before you know it, you've stopped moving — not because God said wait, but because insecurity said you're not enough. But let me tell you something, beloved — fear is a liar, and comparison is a trap. They both exist to keep you from walking boldly in the unique purpose God designed just for you.

## ❖ Fear Paralyzes, But Faith Propels

Fear will always come disguised as wisdom. It'll tell you to "be careful," "wait for a better time," or "maybe this isn't God." But fear's goal isn't to protect you, it's to pause your purpose. "For God has not given us a spirit of fear, but of power, love, and a sound mind." — 2 Timothy 1:7 That means fear is not your portion...Power is.

When fear tells you to hide, faith tells you to move. When fear says, "What if you fail?" faith says, "What if it works?" Every woman God used in Scripture had to confront fear before she stepped into purpose.

• Esther had to face fear to stand before the king.

• Deborah had to lead when others hesitated.

• Mary had to say "yes" when the world would never understand. Fear is not the absence of faith...it's the testing ground of it. Courage isn't doing it without fear — it's doing it in spite of fear.

## ❖ Comparison Kills Confidence

Comparison is one of the enemy's favorite weapons. It will have you measuring your journey against someone else's highlighted reel. But here's the truth: You can't compare seasons you haven't lived. You don't know the price they paid for their oil. You don't know the battles behind their breakthrough. God gave you a specific journey, a specific timing, and a specific anointing.

When you compare your path to someone else's, you insult the creativity of your Creator. "Let each one examine his own work, and then he will have rejoicing in himself alone, and not in another." (Galatians 6:4) You were never meant to be a copy. You were created to be a light...unique, radiant, and unmatched in purpose.

## ❖ You Are Called for Such a Time as This

Don't miss your moment trying to mimic someone else's. The world doesn't need another version of her — it needs the authentic you. The healed you. The bold you. The you that believes again. You don't have to sound like her, look like her, or move like her. God anointed your voice for a reason.

There is a generation attached to your obedience. When you move in fear, you delay them...when you move in faith, you deliver them. "Who knows if perhaps you were made queen for such a time as this?" (Esther 4:14) This is your time, woman of God. Step into it without apology.

## ❖ Practical Ways to Break Free

1. Catch Comparison Early. When you start to measure yourself, pause and thank God for what He's doing in you.

2. Feed Your Faith Daily.  Replace fearful thoughts with Scripture.

3. Celebrate Others.  Someone else's success doesn't threaten yours; it confirms what's possible.

4. Remember Your "Why". Fear loses power when you stay focused on your divine assignment.

### ❖ Prayer of Activation

Father, I thank you for creating me with purpose and uniqueness. Deliver me from the spirit of fear and the trap of comparison. Help me to walk boldly in the path You've prepared for me. Remind me that I am enough because You are in me. I choose faith over fear, authenticity over comparison, and courage over comfort. In Jesus' mighty name, Amen.

### ❖ Declaration of Power

I am free from fear and comparison. I walk in confidence, knowing I am chosen and anointed by God. I celebrate others while embracing my own divine path. I am bold, fearless, and fully aligned with God's timing for my life.

### ❖ Closing Thought

Fear may knock at your door, but faith has the final word. Comparison may try to distract you, but purpose will keep you focused. Walk boldly because the world is waiting for your light.

# My Personal Notes

# Chapter Four

## *Activate Your Anointing*

Every believer carries an anointing...a divine enablement from God to do what ordinary strength cannot. It's not reserved for pastors, prophets, or preachers. It's for every child of God who says, "Yes, Lord, use me."

The anointing isn't just oil poured on the head; it's power poured into the heart. It's the invisible force that gave you courage when you should have crumbled, peace when you should have panicked, and wisdom beyond your years. You were created to operate under Heaven's power, not human pressure. But to do that, you must learn to activate your anointing.

## ❖ What Is the Anointing?

The anointing is "God's divine presence resting upon you to accomplish His will." It's the partnership between your obedience and His power. "It is God who enables us, along with you, to stand firm for Christ. He has commissioned us, and He has identified us as His own by placing the Holy Spirit in our hearts." (2 Corinthians 1:21–22)

The anointing is Heaven's fingerprint on your life; it marks you as chosen, called, and covered. It empowers you to do what seems impossible. When David was first anointed, he was still a shepherd boy. But that oil marked the start of his transformation. The same oil that found him in the field carried him to the throne. You may still feel like you're in the "field" season – unseen, overlooked, or underappreciated, but don't despise it. That's where the anointing grows.

## ❖ Your Anointing Needs Activation

A gift left unopened is useless. The same goes for the anointing. It must be activated through faith, obedience, and surrender. Three keys to activate your anointing are:

1. Obedience.   God's power flows where there is obedience. When He says go, forgive, or speak, your "yes" unlocks His strength. "If you are willing and obedient, you will eat the good things of the land." (Isaiah 1:19)

2. Purity.   The anointing doesn't dwell in chaos or compromise. A pure heart invites a powerful flow. Ask God to cleanse every area that hinders His Spirit.

3. Prayer and Worship.   The anointing increases in the secret place. Every great move of God begins with a surrendered heart. When you worship, you align your spirit with Heaven's rhythm.

4.

## ❖ You're Not Ordinary — You're Appointed

The enemy wants you to think you're just another face in the crowd. But God wants you to know — you carry Heaven's assignment. That's why you can't quit. That's why every attack came so strong…because your anointing threatens darkness.

"The Spirit of the Lord is upon me, because He has anointed me…" (Luke 4:18)

The same Spirit that anointed Jesus now dwells in you. You don't need a stage to be anointed. You just need to surrender.

When you speak words of healing to someone broken, that's the anointing. When you pray for your children through tears, that's the anointing. When you forgive what tried to destroy you, that's the anointing.

### ❖ Protect the Oil

Your anointing is precious — guard it. Not everyone will understand it, and not every space deserves it. Be discerning about what and who you allow to drain your spirit. Oil flows best in vessels that are clean and full of humility. Stay before God and stay teachable; and He will keep filling you again and again.

The more you pour out in service, the more He pours into you through grace. Never forget you are Heaven's vessel, chosen to carry His glory on earth.

### ❖ Prayer of Activation

Father, I thank You for anointing me for a divine purpose. I surrender every fear, doubt, and distraction that hinders Your flow in my life. Fill me afresh with Your Spirit, ignite my faith, and strengthen my obedience. Teach me to walk in humility, power, and boldness. Let Your anointing break every chain that surrounds me and overflow into every life I touch. In Jesus' mighty name, Amen.

### ❖ Declaration of Power

I am anointed and appointed by God. His power flows through me to heal, restore, and uplift others. I am not ordinary; I carry divine oil for a divine assignment. I walk in obedience, purity, and purpose, and I will not waste my anointing

❖ Closing Thought

Your anointing isn't about being seen, it's about being sent. You were chosen for this time, this season, and this mission. Activate your anointing...the world is waiting for your oil to

# Chapter Five

## *From Brokenness to Boldness*

Every powerful woman of faith has walked through a season of brokenness; not the kind that weakens her, but the kind that reshapes her. The kind that teaches her how to fight, how to pray, and how to stand when everything inside wants to fall apart.

Brokenness is not the end of your story; it's the beginning of your transformation. It's the place where God takes what was shattered and turns it into something sacred. You may have walked through betrayal, rejection, or loss but here you are still standing. That alone is proof that grace is greater than pain and purpose is stronger than the wound.

❖ **God Does His Best Work in Broken Places**

When you think of brokenness, you may think

of failure. But in the Kingdom, brokenness is often the doorway to breakthrough. "The Lord is close to the brokenhearted and saves those who are crushed in spirit." (Psalm 34:18)

When God breaks something, it's never to destroy, it's to multiply. He broke the bread before feeding thousands. He broke the alabaster box before the fragrance filled the room. He allows your heart to break so your worship, wisdom, and witness can reach others. Sometimes the cracks in your life aren't flaws, they're openings for God's glory to shine through.

## ❖ When Life Shatters Your Confidence

We all reach moments when life hits so hard that it feels like we'll never recover. The betrayal you didn't see coming. The dream that didn't come true. The door that slammed shut when you were sure God would open it. But even in the rubble, God is still working. He's not replacing the broken pieces; He's rebuilding you stronger than before.

Your brokenness doesn't disqualify you; it qualifies you to carry compassion, humility, and power. It gives you a new depth and a testimony that speaks louder than words ever could. "My grace is sufficient for you, for My power is made perfect in weakness." (2 Corinthians 12:9)

When you stop hiding your scars, you give others permission to heal too.

## ❖ Boldness Is Born from Brokenness

True boldness isn't arrogance; it's confidence rooted in God's faithfulness. It's standing tall after everything has tried to bury you. It's walking into rooms you once felt unworthy to enter, knowing God sent you there.

Every time you rise from pain, you release a roar from Heaven that says,

"I'm still here — and I'm still chosen."

You become a living testimony that the same God who brought you through the fire can bring others out too. Boldness isn't pretending you were never broken — it's declaring, "Yes, I was broken… but I didn't stay there."

❖ Lessons from the Valley

1. Pain reveals your purpose. The enemy attacked you in that area because that's where your anointing flows.

2. Brokenness brings revelation. It teaches you to depend on God like never before.

3. Boldness is your comeback. Every healed wound becomes a weapon of wisdom.

4. Your scars carry glory. Don't hide them, they remind you of where God met you.

❖ Step into Boldness

You have cried enough tears over what was lost. Now it's time to step into what's waiting.

You have been broken yes, but you've also been built. Built to lead. Built to inspire. Built to carry light into dark places. This is your season to stand tall even if your knees are trembling; because boldness isn't the absence of fear, it's the refusal to bow to it. "The righteous are bold as a lion." (Proverbs 28:1)

You are that lioness...powerful, unshaken, and

marked by God.

### ❖ Prayer of Activation

*Father, thank You for meeting me in my brokenness and turning it into strength. I surrender every wound, every disappointment, and every scar to You. Heal what still hurts and ignite boldness in my spirit. Let my testimony bring healing to others. I declare that I will no longer shrink back — I will walk boldly in Your purpose for my life. In Jesus' mighty name, Amen.*

### ❖ Declaration of Power

*I am not broken — I am rebuilt. My scars are proof of God's faithfulness. I walk in courage, confidence, and divine authority. I am bold because the Lion of Judah lives within me.*

### ❖ Closing Thought

You've cried in private — now it's time to stand in power. The same God who met you in your pain will lead you in your purpose. Your brokenness was never meant to end you — it was meant to birth your boldness.

# My Personal Notes

# Chapter Six

## *Faith Over Feelings, Walking in Truth, Not Emotion*

Feelings are powerful. They can lift you one moment and pull you down the next. But as children of God, we are not meant to be led by our feelings — we are meant to be anchored in our faith.

Emotions are real, but they're not always reliable. They fluctuate with circumstances, while faith stands firm on the unchanging Word of God. If you live by how you feel, life will control your peace. But when you live by faith, you control your response, even when life is stormy. "For we walk by faith, not by sight." (2 Corinthians 5:7)

### ❖ When Feelings Speak Louder Than Faith

Let's be honest; some days faith feels far

away. You pray but don't feel God near. You worship but feel nothing changing. You read the Word but still feel weak.

Those are the moments when feelings will tempt you to give up. But faith isn't about feeling God; it's about trusting that He's there even when you don't feel Him. The enemy knows he can't destroy your destiny, so he distracts your emotions. If he can make you live by how you feel, he can keep you from walking by what you know — that God is faithful.

## ❖ Faith Is a Decision, Not a Feeling

Faith says, "I still believe," even when you don't feel strong. Even when your prayers seem unanswered. Even when life doesn't make sense. It's choosing to believe that God's Word is truer than your mood, your fear, or your frustration. "The grass withers, the flower fades, but the word of our God stands forever." (Isaiah 40:8)

Your faith must be rooted in something deeper than emotion. It must be rooted in revelation because revelation doesn't change when circumstances do.

### ❖ The Dangers of Emotional Living

When you live by feelings, you'll:

- Quit when things get hard.

- Doubt when you can't see results.

- Compare circumstances when someone else seems ahead.

- React instead of respond.

### ❖ But when you live by faith, you'll:

- Persevere through pressure.

- Stand firm in uncertainty.

- Rejoice in the waiting.

- Trust the process even when it's painful.

Faith reminds you that God's timing is perfect even when it feels delayed.

Emotions say, "This is too much."

Faith says, "His grace is sufficient for me."

## ❖ How to Strengthen Faith Over Feelings

1. Feed Your Spirit Daily. Faith grows when you stay in God's Word. Your spirit becomes stronger than your emotions.

2. Speak Truth to Yourself. When your feelings say, "I can't," declare, "I can do all things through Christ who strengthens me."

3. Worship Through Worry. Worship changes your focus from "what's" wrong to "who's" in control.

4. Speak Truth to Yourself. When your feelings say, "I can't," you declare, "I can do all things through Christ who strengthens me."

5. Worship Through Worry. Worship changes your focus from "what's" wrong to "who's" in control.

6. Stay Connected. Surround yourself with faith-filled voices such as mentors, pastors, and sisters-in-Christ who remind you of God's truth when your feelings get loud.

## ❖ Even Jesus Felt It

Even Jesus wept. Even He felt alone in Gethsemane. But He didn't let His emotions dictate His obedience. He prayed, "Not My will, but Yours be done."

That's the power of faith surrendering your emotions to God and letting His peace lead your heart.

When you hand your feelings over to Him, He transforms them into fuel for your faith.

## ❖ Prayer of Activation

*Father, I thank You for reminding me that my faith is stronger than my feelings. Help me not to be ruled by emotions but by Your unchanging truth. When my heart is heavy, lift my eyes back to You. When fear speaks, let faith answer. Anchor me in Your Word and teach me to trust You even when I don't understand. I declare that I will walk by faith, not by sight, and that Your peace will rule my heart. In Jesus' name, Amen.*

## ❖ Declaration of Power

*I am not ruled by emotions — I am led by faith. My feelings may change, but God's Word never does. I choose peace over panic, faith over fear, and truth over lies. I walk confidently in the promises of God knowing He is in control.*

## ❖ Closing Thought

Your feelings may waver, but your foundation doesn't have to. When you let faith lead, peace follows. When peace rules, you'll discover that no storm — not even the one within - can shake the power of God inside you.

# My Personal Notes

# Chapter Seven

## *Purpose Over Pain, Turning Your Wounds Into Wisdom*

Pain is a teacher most of us never want, yet it teaches lessons we can't learn any other way. It refines. It humbles. It reveals. And when surrendered to God, pain becomes the very thing that propels us into purpose.

Every scar tells a story of survival. Every tear has watered a seed of strength. You may not have understood why you were suffering at the time, but God was using it to shape your destiny, not destroy it.

"And we know that all things work together for good to those who love God, to those who are called according to His purpose." (Romans 8:28)

### ❖ Pain is a Tool, not a Punishment

God never wastes pain. He uses it as a tool to build endurance, compassion, and spiritual depth. Pain reveals where we still need healing and reminds us that without Him, we can do nothing.

When Joseph was betrayed by his brothers, sold into slavery, and thrown into prison, it looked like pain was winning. But God was positioning him for the palace.

Your suffering is not random; it's refining you for assignment. Before God promotes, He prepares; and preparation often feels like breaking before it feels like a blessing. When you shift your perspective from, "Why me?" to "What is God teaching me?" you begin to walk in purpose instead of pity.

## ❖ The Breaking That Builds You

Sometimes, God allows certain things to break so that something greater can be built. He breaks pride to build humility. He breaks comfort to birth courage. He breaks attachments that keep you from His best.

"Unless a grain of wheat falls to the ground and dies, it remains alone; but if it dies, it produces much fruit." (John 12:24)

There's fruit hidden in your pain — wisdom that will feed others. Your tears were not wasted; they watered the very soil of your next season.

## ❖ Turning Wounds into Wisdom

Wisdom doesn't come from success; it comes from survival. It's what you gain when you look back at pain and realize it didn't break you; it built you. Ask yourself:

• What did that heartbreak teach me about love?

• What did that betrayal teach me about discernment?

• What did that loss teach me about God's faithfulness?

Every wound can either make you bitter or make you wiser; the choice is yours. Let your past become a classroom, not a prison.

## ❖ Your Pain Has a Purpose

The pain that once silenced you is the same pain God will use to give you a voice. You are not the victim of your story...you are the vessel of His glory. You survived so that someone else could believe survival is possible. You endured so that someone else could find hope. You walked through the fire so that others could see that faith still works. "You intended to harm me, but God intended it for good." (Genesis 50:20)

The same people and situations that tried to break you became the foundation God used to build your testimony.

## ❖ The Ministry of Pain

Your ministry is often born from your misery. Your message is often born from your mess, and your purpose is often revealed through your pressure. You are carrying something powerful inside of you — and pain was the midwife that helped deliver it. When you embrace that truth, you no longer run from pain — you learn from it. You begin to walk in purpose over pain.

## ❖ Prayer of Activation

*Father, Thank You for turning my pain into*

*purpose and my wounds into wisdom. I surrender every hurt, every disappointment, and every scar into Your hands. Use them for Your glory, Lord. Help me to see my struggles not as setbacks but as steppingstones to destiny. Teach me to walk in peace, knowing that nothing in my life has been wasted. In Jesus' mighty name, Amen.*

### ❖ Declaration of Power

*My pain has purpose. My wounds carry wisdom. I am not what I went through. I am what God brought me through. Every struggle is shaping me into the woman God designed me to be. I will rise with strength, walk with confidence, and shine with purpose.*

### ❖ Closing Thought

Your story isn't just about what hurt you — it's also about what healed you. The same pain that once broke you will one day become your platform because in God's hands, every wound becomes a weapon of wisdom that changes lives.

# My Personal Notes

# Chapter Eight

## *Becoming "Her", the Woman God Designed You to Be*

There comes a sacred point in every woman's journey when she realizes she's not who she used to be — but she's not quite who she's becoming. It's a divine in-between, a holy transition, where God is reshaping her heart, her habits, and her vision.

Becoming "her" isn't about perfection. It's about transformation. It's about allowing God to strip away the old layers of fear, doubt, and insecurity so that the woman He designed can finally emerge.

You don't become her overnight — you grow into her. Every storm, every prayer, every season of waiting is molding you into the woman who walks in confidence, peace, and divine authority.

"Therefore, if anyone is in Christ, (she) is a new creation; the old has gone, the new has come." — 2 Corinthians 5:17

### ❖ Becoming Her in the Waiting

We often think "becoming" happens in the spotlight — when doors open, dreams manifest, or prayers are answered. But true transformation happens in the waiting room. It's in the hidden seasons where God does His deepest work. He teaches you to trust Him when you can't trace Him. He refines your character when no one is clapping for you. He prepares you for the promise before letting you hold it.

The waiting isn't punishment, it's preparation. God is building her in the background.

### ❖ Becoming Her Through Surrender

To become who God designed you to be, you must be willing to let go of who you thought you were supposed to be. Becoming requires surrender. It means releasing control and letting the Holy Spirit take the lead.

"Not my will, but Yours be done." — Luke

22:42

You can't hold onto your comfort and your calling at the same time. The woman you're becoming requires a new level of trust, forgiveness, discipline, and humility. Every time you choose obedience over opinion, you're stepping closer to her.

### ❖ Becoming Her in Purpose

When you walk in purpose, you no longer chase validation; you move in conviction. You don't compete with others; you complete what God started in you.

The woman God designed you to be doesn't move from insecurity; she moves from identity. She's not defined by applause or approval; she's anchored in assignment.

She carries peace in chaos, wisdom in uncertainty, and grace in transition. She doesn't need to be perfect; she just needs to be present in what God is doing. "She is clothed with strength and dignity, and she laughs without fear of the future." — Proverbs 31:25

That's the woman you are becoming.

## ❖ The Process of Becoming

Becoming "her" is not easy — it's sacred. It will require:

- Healing from what hurt you.
- Forgiving what or who wounded you.
- Believing what God says about you.
- Obeying when it doesn't make sense.

There will be days when you question your progress, but even on those days, you're still becoming. Transformation isn't about how far you've gone, but how surrendered you've become. You're not behind. You're being built.

## ❖ She Already Lives in You

The woman God designed you to be is not a stranger — she's already inside you. Every time you choose faith over fear, she steps forward. Every time you choose peace over panic, she breathes a little freer. Every time you choose prayer over pride, she stands a little taller.

You are not becoming someone new — you're becoming who you've always been in God's eyes. He saw "her" long before you saw yourself.

### ❖ Prayer of Activation

*Father, thank You for the woman I am becoming in You. Help me to surrender fully so You can shape me completely. Remove everything in me that doesn't reflect Your glory. Teach me patience in the process, peace in the waiting, and power in obedience. I trust that every season is molding me into the woman You created me to be. In Jesus' mighty name, Amen.*

### ❖ Declaration of Power

*I am becoming the woman God designed me to be. I am healed, whole, and growing in grace. I release the old and embrace the new. I am confident, fearless, and filled with purpose. The woman within me is rising — strong, radiant, and unstoppable in Christ.*

### ❖ Closing Thought

You are not behind; you're in process. Becoming takes time, but every day you surrender, you evolve. Don't rush the process — embrace it because the woman you are becoming will change everything.

# My Personal Notes

# Chapter Nine

## *When the Fire Refines, Not Destroys*

Every believer eventually faces a fire...a season so intense it feels like everything familiar is melting away. It could be the loss of a loved one, betrayal by someone trusted, or a season where nothing seems to make sense.

You pray, but the heavens feel silent. You believe, yet the breakthrough delays. You show up strong, but inside you're burning. It's easy to think the fire came to destroy you but in truth, it came to refine you. "For You, O God, have tested us; You have refined us as silver is refined." — Psalm 66:10

### ❖ Refinement Has a Purpose

When a silversmith refines silver, he places it in intense heat, not to destroy it, but to remove every impurity. He watches closely, never leaving it unattended, and only removes it when he can see his reflection clearly in the metal. That's exactly what God does with you. He allows the heat, not because He's absent, but because He's present shaping you into His image.

The fire isn't meant to consume you; it's meant to clarify who you truly are. "When you walk through the fire, you will not be burned; the flames will not set you ablaze." — Isaiah 43:2

You may be in the fire, but you are not "of" it. The same flames that burned your comfort are building your character.

## ❖ The Fire Reveals What's Real

Fire exposes what can stay and what must go. It burns away the shallow things: pride, fear, people-pleasing, and dependency on what was never meant to sustain you.

In the fire, you find out:

- Who your true friends are.

- What your real priorities are.

- How much of your strength truly comes from God.

It's in the fire that you stop performing and start transforming.

The woman you were before the fire won't survive where God is taking you next. She was built for safety, but you are being built for strength.

## ❖ God Walks With You in the Fire

When the three Hebrew boys Shadrach, Meshach, and Abednego were thrown into the fiery furnace, the king then saw four men walking in the flames. "Look! I see four men loose, walking in the midst of the fire, and they are not hurt; and the form of the fourth is like the Son of God." — Daniel 3:25

God didn't keep them from the fire; He stepped into it with them. That's how faithful He is. The same Jesus who stood with them, stands with you. You are not alone in your flames. You are walking with the Fire Himself — and that's why you won't burn.

## ❖ The Refining Produces Glory

Refinement is never wasted. Every time you pass through a fire you emerge more radiant, more resilient, more refined in purpose. The heat you feel right now is not punishment, it's preparation. God is burning away what cannot go with you into your next season.

Soon you'll look back and say, "It was good that I was afflicted, because it taught me who God really is."

"After you have suffered a little while, the God of all grace... will Himself restore, confirm, strengthen, and establish you." — 1 Peter 5:10

## ❖ You Are Fireproof in Faith

The enemy thought the fire would destroy you, but it only deepened your worship. He thought it would silence you, but it only sharpened your voice. He thought you'd break, but you burned brighter instead.

Your endurance is your evidence that the hand of God is on your life. The flames refined you, but grace sustained you.

Now you carry a glow that only comes from the fire you survived.

### ❖ Prayer of Activation

*Father, thank You for the refining fire that purifies my heart and strengthens my spirit. When life gets hot, remind me that You are with me in every flame. Burn away everything that's not like You and let Your image shine through me. I surrender to Your process Lord; refine me, use me, and glorify Yourself through my story. In Jesus' mighty name, Amen.*

### ❖ Declaration of Power

*I am refined, not destroyed. The fire did not break me, it built me. God is with me in every flame and His glory shines through my life. What was meant to consume me has only made me stronger. I walk out of the fire radiant, powerful, and unshaken.*

❖ Closing Thought

Don't fear the fire — thank God for it. The same flames that tried to destroy you became the very place where God revealed His power. You are not burning — you're becoming pure gold.

# My Personal Notes

_______________________________________________

_______________________________________________

_______________________________________________

_______________________________________________

_______________________________________________

_______________________________________________

_______________________________________________

_______________________________________________

_______________________________________________

_______________________________________________

_______________________________________________

_______________________________________________.

# Chapter Ten

## *The Voice of Purpose Hearing God's Direction for Your Next Season*

There's a moment in every believer's journey when God begins to whisper, "It's time. Time to move forward. Time to step into the new. Time to leave behind what no longer serves your growth."

But often, His voice doesn't come through thunder or lightning; it comes through a still, gentle whisper. If your heart is crowded with noise, fear, and confusion, you can miss the voice.

Purpose doesn't shout; it calls. And when it calls, everything in your spirit begins to awaken.

"Your ears shall hear a word behind you, saying, 'This is the way, walk in it.'" — Isaiah 30:21

### ❖ Learning to Hear the Voice of Purpose

The voice of purpose isn't always easy to

discern because it rarely aligns with comfort. God's direction will often pull you away from what feels safe and into what requires faith.

Purpose says, "Go." Fear says, "Stay." But the moment you obey the whisper of God, doors begin to open that no man can shut.

God doesn't speak to your fear, He speaks to your future. So, if what you're hearing is leading you toward peace, faith, and growth, that's Him. "My sheep hear My voice, and I know them, and they follow Me." — John 10:27

### ❖ The Noise That Drowns Out God's Voice

Sometimes we can't hear God, not because He's silent, but because we're distracted. The noise of busyness, worry, and comparison drowns out His whisper.

Before you can hear Him clearly, you have to quiet the voices competing for your attention. That means silencing:

- The voice of fear that says, "You'll fail."

- The voice of people that says, "You're not ready."

- The voice of doubt that says, "You're not enough."

When you make space for stillness, Heaven begins to speak.

God's instructions are often gentle but weighty. They carry peace, not pressure.

## ❖ Recognizing the Signs of a New Season

Purpose always announces itself before it manifests. You'll begin to feel a shift, a stirring in your spirit that says, "There's more."

You'll notice:

- The things that once satisfied no longer do.

- The people who used to fit your life start to drift.

- The opportunities that come align more with your assignment than your ambition. These are signs that God is positioning you for your next season.

He will never move you without first preparing your heart. So, if you feel the tension, it's not rejection, it's redirection. "Behold, I am doing a new thing; now it springs forth, do you not perceive it?" — Isaiah 43:19

### ❖ Obedience Is the Language of Purpose

Hearing God's voice is one thing; following it is another. Purpose demands obedience even when you don't have all the answers.

When God told Abraham to leave his homeland, He didn't give him a map, just a promise. Faith walks without seeing the full picture.

Every act of obedience is a seed. Those seeds produce harvests you couldn't imagine. So, when God says go, move. When He says wait, trust. When He says forgive, obey, because every yes draws you closer to destiny.

## ❖ Walking in Clarity and Confidence

God's voice will never confuse you; it will clarify you. It will bring light where there was fog, strength where there was doubt, and peace where there was fear. You don't need to have all the details to take the next step. All you need is confidence in the One who is directing your path.

"Trust in the Lord with all your heart and lean not on your own understanding; in all your ways acknowledge Him, and He shall direct your paths." — Proverbs 3:5-6

When you walk with God, uncertainty becomes an adventure not an obstacle.

## ❖ Prayer of Activation

*Father, thank You for speaking purpose and direction into my life. Help me to recognize Your voice above all others. Quiet every distraction, fear, and doubt that tries to cloud my clarity. Teach me to walk in obedience, even when the path is unfamiliar. I trust that Your plans for me are good and that You are leading me into my next season with peace and confidence. In Jesus' mighty name, Amen.*

### ❖ Declaration of Power

*I hear God's voice clearly and walk boldly in His direction. I am no longer confused, anxious, or afraid. God's purpose is unfolding in my life with power and precision. Every step I take is ordered, anointed, and aligned with Heaven's plan.*

### ❖ Closing Thought

Purpose doesn't always begin with clarity — it begins with obedience. The moment you say "Yes" to God's whisper, the rest will unfold in His perfect timing. You are walking into your next season — not lost but led.

# My Personal Notes

# Chapter Eleven

## *Rise and Reign Walking in Spiritual Authority and Confidence*

There comes a moment when a woman who once doubted herself finally looks in the mirror and sees what Heaven always saw...a daughter of the King, chosen and crowned by grace.

She's no longer begging for permission to be powerful. She's walking in it.

She's not seeking validation from people; she's standing in revelation from God. She's not afraid of rejection because she's accepted in the Beloved.

This is what it means to rise and reign. It's not pride, it's identity. It's not arrogance, it's awareness of who you are in Christ. "But you are a chosen generation, a royal priesthood, a holy nation, His own special people." — 1 Peter 2:9

## ❖ The Authority Within You

When you gave your life to Christ, you didn't just receive salvation, you received authority:

- ❖ To trample on fear.
- ❖ To silence lies.
- ❖ To shift atmospheres with your words and prayers.

"Behold, I give you the authority to trample on serpents and scorpions, and over all the power of the enemy." --- Luke 10:19

You carry Heaven's permission to live boldly. You don't need to wait for someone to approve what God has already anointed.

The enemy knows your authority; that's why he works overtime to make sure you forget it.

But it's time to remember who you are. You are not defeated; you are divinely and royally clothed in victory.

## ❖ Confidence Rooted in Christ

True confidence doesn't come from appearance, possessions, or status. It comes from identity in Christ. Confidence says:

- "I am who God says I am."
- "I have what God says I have."
- "I can do what God says I can do."

When you know who you are, insecurity loses its grip. Your worth is no longer negotiable; it's established by Heaven.

Even on your worst days, you are still chosen, still loved, still powerful.

"Being confident of this very thing, that He who began a good work in you will carry it on to completion." — Philippians 1:6

### ❖ Rising After Rejection

Every queen has faced rejection before her reign. David was overlooked before he was crowned. Joseph was betrayed before he was promoted. Esther was orphaned before she was enthroned.

Rejection isn't the end; it's often the redirection that leads you to your royal position.

You don't need everyone to believe in you

when God has already chosen you. Your crown fits whether they recognize it or not.

Rejection refines your focus. It teaches you that your value doesn't decrease because someone else couldn't see it.

## ❖ Walking in Spiritual Authority

Spiritual authority isn't about control, it's about influence. It's when Heaven backs your words because they align with God's will.

When you speak peace, storms calm. When you declare healing, hearts shift. When you pray in faith, chains break.

That's not wishful thinking — that's the power of divine authority. To walk in that authority, you must stay connected to the Source. Intimacy with God is the key to sustaining influence.

"Submit yourselves, then, to God. Resist the devil, and he will flee from you." — James 4:7

Submission unlocks strength. Humility unlocks power. Obedience unlocks authority.

### ❖ How to Rise and Reign Daily

1. Start your day in the Word. — It reminds you who you are before the world tells you who you're not.

2. Speak life out loud. — Your words shape your world; declare victory before you see it.

3. Walk with posture. — Royalty doesn't shrink; stand tall in grace and confidence.

4. Stay humble and grateful. — True queens serve with compassion and lead with love.

You're not rising to dominate others — you're rising to lift others higher.

### ❖ Prayer of Activation

*Father, thank you for calling me chosen, royal, and anointed. Teach me to walk in the authority and confidence that comes from You. Help me to rise from fear, shame, and limitation into bold faith and purpose. Let my life reflect Your power, humility, and grace. I declare that I am not defeated — I am crowned with favor and purpose. In Jesus' mighty name, Amen.*

❖ Declaration of Power

*I rise with boldness and reign with grace. I am a daughter of the King, clothed in strength and dignity. My confidence is rooted in Christ, not in circumstances. I walk in divine authority, speak with power, and live with purpose.*

❖ Closing Thought

You are not a victim of your past; you are the victor of your purpose. You don't just survive, you reign. Walk like royalty, speak like victory and live like Heaven's representative on earth. That's who you've always been, chosen to rise and reign.

# My Personal Notes

# Chapter Twelve

## *The Power of A Transformed Mind Living Free From Limiting Thoughts*

Everything begins in the mind. Before a person speaks defeat, she thinks defeat. Before she gives up, she believes there's no point in trying. Before she fears, she imagines failure.

That's why the battlefield of faith isn't around you, it's within you. The enemy doesn't have to take your future if he can capture your thoughts. But God's Word declares that transformation happens from the inside out.

"Do not be conformed to this world but be transformed by the renewing of your mind." — Romans 12:2

Your mind determines your movement. If your thinking is small, your faith will be small. But if your thoughts are renewed by truth, your life will expand to match Heaven's vision for you.

### ❖ The Mind Is the Gateway

Your mind is the doorway between your faith and your future. Every thought that enters either builds you or breaks you.

That's why the Bible tells us to take every thought captive (2 Corinthians 10:5).

You are not meant to entertain every idea, fear, or insecurity that enters your mind — you have the authority to reject it.

You can't always control what thoughts appear, but you can control which ones you allow to stay.

When a thought says, "You'll never be enough," respond with, "I am fearfully and wonderfully made."

When a thought says, "It's too late for me," declare, "God makes all things new." When a thought says, "You're alone," proclaim, "God is with me always."

The mind follows whatever voice you feed it.

### ❖ Renewing the Mind Daily

Transformation doesn't happen in a single moment; it happens in daily surrender. Renewing your mind means consistently replacing lies with truth until truth becomes your reflex.

Here's how to start:

1. Start your mornings in the Word. It sets the tone for your thoughts before the world can.

2. Practice gratitude. Thankfulness reprograms your focus toward God's goodness.

3. Guard your atmosphere. Be careful what voices, music, and media you allow into your spirit.

4. Affirm the Word out loud. Speaking Scripture strengthens faith and silences fear.

"Set your minds on things above, not on earthly things." — Colossians 3:2

A renewed mind doesn't just think differently — it lives differently.

### ❖ Breaking Free from Limiting Beliefs

Many of us are living below God's potential, not because of a lack of power, but because of limiting beliefs. We've told ourselves:

- "I'm too old."

- "I'm too broken."

- "I'm not qualified."

But God specializes in using the unexpected, the underestimated, and the unqualified. Moses had a stutter, David had a past, and Esther had no status. Yet all three of them changed history. The only limit on your life is the one you've accepted in your mind.

It's time to let go of small thinking and start believing in a big God.

## ❖ God's Thoughts About You

The most powerful transformation happens when you start thinking about yourself the way God thinks about you.

He says:

- You are loved. (Jeremiah 31:3)

- You are chosen. (John 15:16)

- You are forgiven. (Isaiah 43:25)

- You are powerful. (Ephesians 3:20)

When you align your thoughts with His truth, everything in your life begins to shift your peace, your confidence, your direction, and your destiny. The renewed mind doesn't chase validation; it carries revelation.

## ❖ Protecting Your Peace

A transformed mind is a guarded mind. Not every battle is yours to fight, and not every voice deserves your response.

Protect your peace like it's sacred because it is. Peace is proof of presence. When you feel anxious, don't assume God is far...assume your focus has drifted.

Return to the Word, worship, and stillness. That's where your mind resets and your spirit realigns.

"You will keep in perfect peace those whose minds are stayed on You." — Isaiah 26:3

## ❖ Prayer of Activation

*Father, renew my mind daily with Your truth.*

Break every stronghold of fear, doubt, and insecurity that limits my growth. Replace old thoughts with new revelations. Help me to see myself and my future through Your eyes. Let my thoughts align with Heaven, and let my mind become a place of peace, power, and clarity. In Jesus' mighty name, Amen.

### ❖ Declaration of Power

My mind is renewed and my spirit is free. I no longer think small, live afraid, or dwell in doubt. I have the mind of Christ - s t r o n g, focused, and full of peace. My thoughts agree with God's Word and my life reflects His truth.

### ❖ Closing Thought

Transformation starts with a thought and a decision to believe what God says above all else. When your mind changes, your life follows. You don't need a new reality — you need a renewed mindset. The greatest power is already within you.

# My Personal Notes

# Chapter Thirteen

## *When God Seems Silent, Trusting His Timing in the Waiting*

There will be seasons in your walk with God when Heaven feels quiet. You pray, but no answer comes. You cry out, but all you hear is stillness. You ask for directions, but every door seems to stay shut.

It's in those moments that your faith is truly tested, not in the noise of miracles, but in the silence of waiting.

But silence does not mean absence. God's quiet seasons are often where He does His most careful work.

"Be still and know that I am God." — Psalm 46:10

❖ **The Silence Is Not Punishment — It's Preparation**

When God is silent, He is never still. Behind

the scenes, He's aligning people, timing, and circumstances in ways you can't yet see.

Think of Joseph who was sold, betrayed, and imprisoned yet in that silence, God was preparing the throne. Think of Hannah weeping in prayer yet her silence birthed a prophet. Think of Jesus silent in the grave yet resurrection was already on schedule.

The waiting room is not a wasted room. It's where faith matures, trust deepens, and vision becomes clear.

### ❖ Faith in the Quiet

Faith is not proven in answered prayers; it's proven in delayed ones. Anyone can trust God when the answer comes quickly. But true faith is trusting when you don't understand the timing.

You may not see it, but God is writing something eternal through your patience.

"For still the vision awaits its appointed time… If it seems slow, wait for it; it will surely come; it will not delay." — Habakkuk 2:3

Your waiting season is not a sign that God forgot you — it's a sign that He's preparing something worth waiting for.

### ❖ What to Do While You Wait

1. Worship Instead of Worry. Every time you feel anxious, turn that energy into praise. Worship reminds you that God is still in control.

2. Stay Faithful in the Small Things. Keep serving, praying, and doing what's in front of you. Sometimes your next level is hidden in your current obedience.

3. Watch Your Words. Speak life even when you can't see life. Your words carry power even in the quiet.

4. Write Down the Promises. Keep a journal of what God spoke before the silence — because when He speaks again, it will connect every dot. "Blessed is she who has believed that the Lord would fulfill His promises to her." — Luke 1:45

### ❖ The Silence Is Where Strength Is Born

You will find strength in the stillness that crowds could never give you. Because when everything goes quiet, that's when you finally hear your own spirit say, "Even if He doesn't, I still trust Him." It's in those moments that your relationship with God becomes personal — not just based on blessings, but on belief.

The silence is not empty — it's sacred. It's where God builds your endurance for what's ahead.

### ❖ When the Wait Turns into Worship

One day, the silence will break. The promise will come, and you'll realize that every tear you cried was watering the ground of your miracle.

You'll look back and say, "It was good for me that I was afflicted, so that I might learn Your decrees." — Psalm 119:71

Waiting seasons teach us that God's timeline is perfect, even when it's painful.

The moment you stop fighting the silence and start worshiping in it, peace replaces frustration.

### ❖ Prayer of Activation

*Father, thank You for being present even when I cannot hear You. Teach me to trust You in the silence and rest in Your perfect timing. Calm my anxious thoughts and help me wait with expectation instead of fear. Strengthen my faith to believe that You are working all things together for my good. Let my heart be still and my worship stay strong as I wait on You. In Jesus' mighty name, Amen.*

### ❖ Declaration of Power

*I am not forgotten. God is working even when I cannot see it. I will wait in faith, worship in patience, and trust in peace. My waiting season is preparing me for my winning season. The silence is not the end; it's the setup for something greater.*

❖ Closing Thought

Heaven's silence is never God's absence. It's the sacred pause before the promise unfolds. Wait well, daughter of God — because when He finally speaks, everything will make sense.

# My Personal Notes

# Chapter Fourteen

## *Peace Over Pressure Finding Rest in a World That Never Stops*

We live in a world that glorifies hustle, noise, and constant movement. It tells you that if you're not busy, you're falling behind; that rest is weakness; and slowing down means losing momentum. But the Kingdom of God operates differently. God's greatest work in you happens not when you're running, but when you're resting.

Peace is not the absence of problems; it's the presence of God in the middle of them. Sometimes, peace means learning to say no to pressure and yes to presence.

"Come to Me, all you who are weary and burdened, and I will give you rest." — Matthew 11:28

### ❖ The Pressure to Perform

Pressure whispers, "Do more. Be more. Prove

more." It makes you feel like your worth is based on how much you accomplish instead of who you already are. But beloved, you don't have to perform for God — you simply have to be with Him.

You were never called to live burnt out, exhausted, or anxious trying to meet human expectations. Jesus Himself rested. He withdrew from the crowds to pray, to breathe, to refocus. If the Son of God needed rest, so do you.

"In returning and rest you shall be saved; in quietness and confidence shall be your strength." — Isaiah 30:15

When you slow down long enough to sit at His feet, you'll realize that the pressure to be everything was never from Him.

### ❖ Choosing Peace in a Demanding World

Peace is not found when everything calms down — it's found when you calm within. Even in chaos, you can remain centered in God's love.

To choose peace, you must:

1. Protect your boundaries. Not every opportunity is a divine assignment.

2. Prioritize presence. Make time daily to sit quietly with God — even five minutes of silence can reset your soul.

3. Practice gratitude. Gratitude silences anxiety: you can't worry and worship at the same time.

4. Release control. Peace begins where striving ends.

You were not designed to carry the weight of the world — that's God's job.

## ❖ When You Feel Overwhelmed

There will be moments when life feels too heavy with responsibilities, deadlines, expectations, and even ministry work. But remember you can do anything through Christ, but not everything at once.

Peace doesn't come from having control; it comes from trusting that God is in control. You don't need to have every answer; you just need to rest in the One who does.

Sometimes, the most spiritual thing you can do is breathe and to sit in silence and whisper, "Lord, I trust You."

"You will keep in perfect peace those whose minds are stayed on You, because they trust in You." — Isaiah 26:3

### ❖ Peace Is Power

Peace is not passive, it's powerful. It's what allows you to smile in storms, worship under pressure, and think clearly when others panic.

The enemy wants to steal your peace because he knows that once you lose it, you lose focus. But when you guard your peace, you guard your power.

So today, refuse to be rushed, rattled, or reactive. Slow down, breathe deep, and remember - peace is your inheritance.

"My peace I give to you; not as the world gives do I give to you." — John 14:27

### ❖ Rest Is Holy

Rest isn't laziness, it's worship. It says, "God, I trust You enough to stop striving." When you rest, you're telling Heaven, "I believe You'll handle what I can't." That kind of faith invites miracles.

Even the land God created was given rest every seventh year because rest restores everything that's been drained. You deserve that same restoration.

### ❖ Prayer of Activation

*Father, thank You for being my peace in every storm. Teach me to rest in You without guilt or fear. Silence the noise of pressure and let Your presence quiet my heart. Help me to release control and trust that You are working behind the scenes. Fill me with divine peace that surpasses understanding, and let me live from a place of rest, not rush. In Jesus' mighty name, Amen.*

### ❖ Declaration of Power

*I choose peace over pressure. I am not defined*

*by what I do but by who I am in Christ. I release stress, worry, and striving; and I embrace divine rest. I live from a place of calm confidence, knowing God is in control.*

## ❖ Closing Thought

You don't have to keep running to prove you're worthy...you already are. Slow down, breathe deeply, and rest in the rhythm of grace. True peace is not found in doing more, it's found in being still and knowing He is God.

# My Personal Notes

# Chapter Fifteen

## *Walking in Wholeness*
## *Healing Your Heart, Spirit, and Soul*

Wholeness doesn't mean you've never been broken, it means you've allowed God to make you whole again. It means your scars no longer control you, your past no longer defines you, and your heart finally beats in rhythm with peace.

Many people survive life but never truly live again after the pain. They smile on the outside but still bleed on the inside. They worship in public but cry in private.

But God didn't just call you to survive, He called you to be whole.

"Beloved, I pray that you may prosper in all things and be in health, just as your soul prospers." — 3 John 1:2

### ❖ Healing Is a Journey, Not a Moment

Healing doesn't happen in an instant; it

happens in layers. God peels away pain like the layers of an onion...gently, patiently, and with love.

One day you'll wake up and realize that what once broke you no longer defines you. The tears that once represented pain will now represent freedom.

Wholeness means your soul has learned to breathe again.

"He heals the brokenhearted and binds up their wounds." — Psalm 147:3

You don't have to rush the process. Even if healing feels slow, every small step counts; every prayer, every journal entry, and every moment you choose forgiveness over bitterness.

### ❖ Healing Your Heart

A wounded heart often hides behind strength. We say, "I'm fine," when we're really hurting. We stay busy to avoid feeling. But true strength comes from honesty and from letting God touch the places you've been protecting.

Healing begins with permission to feel, to

forgive, and to let go. You can't heal from what you won't face; and you can't release what you keep rehearsing.

When you bring your pain to God, He doesn't shame you, He soothes you. He doesn't just patch your heart; He gives you a new one.

"I will give you a new heart and put a new spirit within you." — Ezekiel 36:26

## ❖ Healing Your Spirit

Your spirit is where God lives, but pain can dim your awareness of His presence. When your spirit feels crushed, you may find it hard to pray, praise, or believe again. But the beautiful thing about God's Spirit is this, He meets you where you are, not where you "should" be.

He breathes life back into dry places. He revives your faith when you're weary. He reminds you that the same Spirit that raised Jesus from the dead lives inside of you.

You are never too broken to be used, never too wounded to be healed. Every crushed place is a candidate for His glory.

## ❖ Healing Your Soul

Your soul is the seat of your emotions, memories, and identity. Sometimes the soul holds onto pain long after the event has passed. That's why healing requires renewal through exchanging old thoughts for God's truth.

Forgiveness becomes the bridge to freedom. You're not excusing what happened, you're releasing yourself from its grip.

Your soul finds peace when it stops reliving the past and starts embracing the present. Every day you choose joy, gratitude, and faith, you strengthen your soul's foundation.

"Why, my soul, are you downcast? Put your hope in God." — Psalm 42:11

## ❖ Wholeness Is a Lifestyle

Walking in wholeness is not about never feeling pain again; it's about knowing where to take it when it comes. It's about guarding your peace, nurturing your spirit, and feeding your faith.

Wholeness means:

- You stop apologizing for healing.
- You forgive yourself for past mistakes.
- You protect what God restored in you.

Every healed woman becomes a healer for others. When you walk in wholeness, your very presence becomes a sanctuary for broken souls.

### ❖ Prayer of Activation

Father, thank You for being the God who restores my soul. Heal every part of me — my heart, my spirit, and my mind. Remove the residue of pain, bitterness, and fear. Fill every space with Your love and peace.

Teach me to walk in wholeness and protect what You've restored in me. I declare that I am healed, whole, and complete in You. In Jesus' mighty name, Amen.

### ❖ Declaration of Power

I am healed and made whole. My past no longer has power over me. My heart is free, my mind is renewed, and my spirit is restored. I live in peace, strength, and divine wholeness every day.

❖ Closing Thought

Wholeness isn't a destination — it's a daily walk with the Healer. You may have been broken, but now you are beautiful, complete, and free. When God restores, He doesn't just fix — He makes all things new.

# My Personal Notes

# Chapter Sixteen

## *Reigniting Your Fire, Staying Spiritually Strong When You Feel Empty*

There are moments in every believer's journey when the fire that once burned bright begins to flicker. You still love God, but you feel tired. You still show up, but something feels dim inside. You still pray, but the words come slower.

It's not that your faith is gone;  it's that your flame needs fresh oil. Even the strongest believers can grow weary. Even those filled with purpose can find themselves running on empty. But the good news is the fire of God can be rekindled.

"Never let the fire in your heart go out. Keep it alive. Serve the Lord." — Romans 12:11 (NCV)

### ❖ Recognizing Spiritual Burnout

Spiritual exhaustion doesn't always look like

rebellion; sometimes it looks like routine. You're doing all the right things but feeling none of the joy. You're pouring into others but haven't been poured into. You're strong for everyone else but silently falling apart inside.

That's not failure, that's fatigue. And it's God's gentle reminder that you need to return to the Source.

Even Jesus withdrew from the crowds to pray and recharge. If the Savior of the world needed rest and renewal, so do you.

### ❖ Return to Your First Love

There's a reason God said to the church in the Book of Revelation:

"You have forsaken the love you had at first." — Revelation 2:4

When your heart starts feeling dry, go back to the beginning. Back to the simple moments when worship felt pure, when prayer wasn't a duty but a delight, and when His presence was your favorite place.

You don't need a new assignment; you need a renewed affection. The fire is not gone; it's waiting to be stirred.

"Therefore, I remind you to fan into flame the gift of God, which is in you." — 2 Timothy 1:6

### ❖ How to Rekindle Your Fire

1. Feed Your Spirit Again. Go back to the Word — not out of obligation, but hunger. Read until your heart feels alive again.

2. Find Stillness. The noise of life often smothers the flame. Silence creates space for the Spirit to breathe.

3. Worship Deeply. Worship breaks chains and rekindles fire. Even when you don't "feel" it, lift your hands...the atmosphere will shift.

4. Surround Yourself with Fire Starters. Spend time with those who ignite your faith, not drain it. Iron sharpens iron.

5. Serve from Overflow, Not Obligation. You can't pour from an empty cup. Fill yourself in

His presence first then pour with joy, not exhaustion.

### ❖ Fresh Oil for a New Season

The same God who lit your fire in the past can fill your lamp again today.

He doesn't just want you to burn for Him once — He wants you to burn for Him always.

Your anointing needs refilling just like a flame needs oil. So come back to the altar — not for show, but for strength.

"But the wise took oil in their vessels with their lamps." — Matthew 25:4

Don't let the flame fade because you're afraid of starting over. Every time you return to Him, the fire burns brighter than before.

### ❖ From Empty to Empowered

You don't have to stay weary; God's presence is the oxygen your spirit needs.

Let Him breathe on you again. Let Him restore your joy, refill your passion, and renew your strength.

When you reconnect to His presence, you won't just survive ministry — you'll thrive in it.

You'll pray with power again. You'll worship with passion again.

You'll love without exhaustion again because His fire never fails — it only waits to be rekindled.

### ❖ Prayer of Activation

Father, thank you for being the fire that never goes out. Forgive me for the times I've run on empty trying to do Your work without Your presence. Today, I return to You — my Source, my Strength, my Flame. Breathe fresh life into me. Reignite my passion, my worship, and my faith. Let my heart burn again for You and let my light shine for Your glory. In Jesus' mighty name, Amen.

### ❖ Declaration of Power

My fire is alive and burning bright. I am not empty — I am filled with the power of the Holy

Spirit. I am refreshed, renewed, and reignited with passion and purpose. The flame within me will never go out because God Himself is my Source.

### ❖ Closing Thought

Your flame didn't die — it just needed air. Breathe again. Worship again. Believe again. The fire within you is coming back stronger than ever — and this time, it will never be extinguished.

# My Personal Notes

# Chapter Seventeen

## *Carrying the Light, Becoming A Vessel of Hope and Influence*

There's something beautiful about a woman who's been through darkness and still carries light. She's not shining because life was easy; she's shining because she discovered what light really is.

You've walked through storms, endured the fire, healed from pain, and reignited your flame. Now it's time to carry that light into a world that desperately needs hope.

"You are the light of the world. A city set on a hill cannot be hidden."

—Matthew 5:14

You were never meant to hide your glow — you were created to illuminate.

### ❖ You Are a Vessel of Light

When God shines through you, it's not for decoration, it's for direction. Your light guides others who are still lost in the dark. Your story becomes a map that leads someone else to freedom. You are a walking testimony and proof that grace still works, healing is possible, and God still restores broken things.

The light you carry is not your own; it's His Spirit within you. And when you let it shine, darkness cannot comprehend it.

"The light shines in the darkness, and the darkness has not overcome it." — John 1:5

### ❖ From Wounds to Witness—Influence

Your scars tell stories that sermons can't. When people see your strength, they see God's faithfulness.

Never be ashamed of your journey; your transparency might be the key to someone else's transformation. You carry light not by being perfect, but by being real.

You've overcome not just for yourself, but for the countless lives attached to your obedience.

When you speak hope into someone's pain,

you release the same power that once healed you. You become a vessel of healing, encouragement, and purpose—a living channel of God's glory.

## ❖ Through Integrity

In a world chasing fame, God is raising women of faithful influence. You don't need a platform to have impact. Your light shines in your home, your workplace, your ministry, and even in quiet acts of kindness.

Influence is not about visibility, it's about consistency. It's when your character speaks louder than your words.

Let your influence flow from intimacy with God. The brighter your private relationship with Him, the stronger your public light will shine.

"Let your light so shine before men, that they may see your good works and glorify your Father in heaven." — Matthew 5:16

## ❖ Keeping the Light Burning

Light requires fuel. If you stop feeding your

spirit, your glow will fade. To keep shining:

1. Stay connected to the Source. Spend daily time in the Word and prayer — that's your oil.

2. Stay humble. Remember that the glory belongs to God, not us.

3. Stay compassionate. Never let success harden your heart.

4. Stay teachable. Light grows brighter through learning and surrender.

Your light was never meant to burn out; it was meant to burn on purpose.

## ❖ Becoming a Beacon of Hope

When others see you shining through adversity, they'll know God is real.

Your peace will preach louder than your words. Your kindness will minister louder than a microphone. Your perseverance will inspire faith in weary souls.

Don't underestimate your presence; light doesn't have to speak to make an impact; it simply shines.

Every time you show love, forgive quickly, or encourage someone else, your light grows stronger. You are a walking reflection of Heaven's hope.


### ❖ Prayer of Activation

Father, thank You for trusting me to carry Your light. Let my life radiate Your love, hope, and truth wherever I go. Use my story to heal hearts and point people back to You. Protect my light from the weight of the world and keep my flame burning with compassion and humility. May everything I do bring glory to Your name. In Jesus' mighty name, Amen.


### ❖ Declaration of Power

I am the light of the world — a vessel of hope and healing. My life shines with God's glory and reflects His goodness. I am not hidden, forgotten, or dimmed. I am radiant with purpose. Everywhere I go, darkness must flee because His light lives in me.

You are not just a survivor — you are a shining example of what God can do through a surrendered heart. So, walk boldly, glow brightly, and carry your light fearlessly. Somewhere, someone is finding their way home by the light that shines from you.

# My Personal Notes

# Chapter Eighteen

## *Becoming Unstoppable, Walking Boldly Into Destiny Without Fear*

There comes a defining moment in every woman's journey when she realizes she is no longer the same. She's not the woman who once doubted herself, cried herself to sleep, or questioned her worth. She's stronger now and wiser; rooted in faith and guided by divine purpose.

This is the moment when transformation becomes movement, when revelation turns into action. This is what it means to become unstoppable.

"The Lord will fulfill His purpose for me; Your love, O Lord, endures forever." — Psalm 138:8

### ❖ Unstoppable Doesn't Mean Unshaken

Being unstoppable doesn't mean life will never

try to break you again. It means that no matter what comes, you will not quit.

You might cry, but you'll keep walking. You might stumble, but you'll rise again. You might be pressed, but you'll never be crushed.

"We are hard pressed on every side but not crushed; perplexed, but not in despair." — 2 Corinthians 4:8

Your strength doesn't come from striving — it comes from staying connected to the One who never fails.

### ❖ Fear Has No Power Over Destiny

Fear will always try to stand at the doorway of your next level. But every time you choose faith instead of fear, you break another barrier.

Fear says, "What if it doesn't work?" Faith says, "What if it does work?"

The truth is, your purpose is more powerful than your past, and your calling is greater than your comfort zone. You are not just stepping into destiny; you are defying every limitation that once tried to hold you back.

"For God has not given us a spirit of fear, but of power and love and a sound mind." — 2 Timothy 1:7

## ❖ Keep Moving Forward

One of the enemy's greatest weapons is distraction — if he can't destroy you, he'll try to delay you. But this is your season to move with focus and fire.

You've cried enough. You've waited enough. Now it's time to act on what God has already confirmed.

When He opens the door, don't second-guess it, walk through. When He gives you the idea, don't shrink back, create it. When He gives you the platform, don't hide, speak with boldness.

The time for hesitation is over. You are not waiting on God anymore. God is waiting on you.

## ❖ Your Destiny Is Bigger Than You

Your destiny is not just about your success;

it's about your significance. There are lives attached to your obedience and generations tied to your "yes."

When you walk in purpose, others find permission to do the same. When you stand in boldness, others find the courage to rise. You are a trailblazer, the one who turns broken roads into pathways of hope.

You were not born to blend in. You were born to stand out and stand firm.

"Arise, shine, for your light has come, and the glory of the Lord rises upon you." — Isaiah 60:1

### ❖ How to Stay Unstoppable

1. Stay grounded in prayer. Power flows from intimacy with God.

2. Stay surrounded by visionaries. Walk with people who challenge your faith, not your focus.

3. Stay humble in victory. The higher God takes you, the deeper your roots in humility must go.

4. Stay consistent. Destiny is not built in

moments of emotion but in decisions of discipline. You can't lose when your heart is aligned with Heaven.

### ❖ Prayer of Activation

Father, thank You for the strength and courage to walk boldly in my purpose. I renounce every fear, doubt, and distraction that tries to keep me small. Fill me with unstoppable faith, divine focus, and supernatural endurance. Lead me to every place You've destined for me and let my life bring You glory. I declare that I am unshakable, unafraid, and unstoppable in You. In Jesus' mighty name, Amen.

### ❖ Declaration of Power

I am unstoppable because God's power lives in me. I walk boldly, fearlessly, and faithfully into my destiny. No weapon formed against me will prosper, and no fear will silence my voice. I was created to rise, to reign, and to fulfill God's purpose for my life.

❖ Closing Thought

You've been broken and rebuilt, tested and trained, refined and restored. Now, it's your time to rise — not timidly, but triumphantly.

Walk boldly, beloved. You've become everything God knew you could be. And now the world will see the unstoppable light of The Power Within you.

# My Personal Notes

# About the Author

*Moira Boakai is a faith leader, author, speaker, and the founder of **Break Free International Ministry,** a global ministry dedicated to helping individuals experience spiritual healing, restoration, and freedom through the power of God.*

Her life journey is a testimony of resilience, faith, and divine restoration. Through seasons of personal hardship, betrayal, and spiritual battles, Moira discovered a deeper relationship with God that transformed her pain into purpose. Rather than allowing life's challenges to silence her, she allowed God to use them as a platform to encourage and uplift others.

**As the author of "The Diary of a Pastor's Wife" and "The Power That Is Within"**, Minister Boakai shares powerful insights about spiritual growth, inner strength, and the transforming power of faith. Her writings inspire readers to  recognize the authority and strength that God has already placed inside of them.

Through **Break Free International Ministry**, she

ministers to people around the world, offering encouragement, prayer, biblical teaching, and empowerment for those seeking breakthrough in their lives.

Moira's mission is simple yet powerful:

***To remind people that the same power that raised Christ from the dead lives within them.***

Her passion is to see individuals rise above their circumstances, walk in their God-given identity, and live a life of purpose, freedom, and victory.